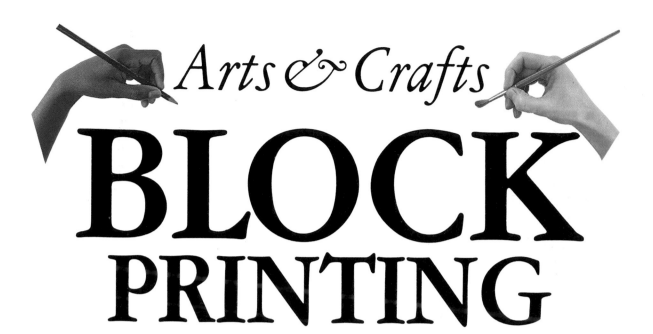

Arts & Crafts
BLOCK PRINTING

Susie O'Reilly

With photographs by Zul Mukhida

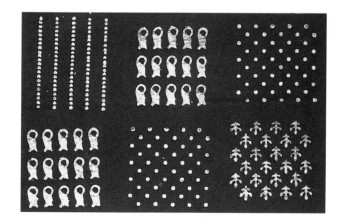

Thomson Learning
New York

Titles in this series

BATIK AND TIE-DYE
BLOCK PRINTING
MODELING
PAPERMAKING
STENCILING
WEAVING

Frontispiece *Detail of a piece of block-printed fabric from India.*

First published in the
United States in 1993 by
Thomson Learning
115 Fifth Avenue
New York, NY 10003

First published in 1993 by
Wayland (Publishers) Ltd

Cataloging-in-Publication Data
applied for

ISBN: 1-56847-065-7

Printed in Italy

CONTENTS

Words printed in **bold** appear in the glossary.

GETTING STARTED

Block printing is an ancient craft. Four thousand years ago, the Egyptians were using carved blocks to print patterns on **fabric**. By the sixth century, the craft was widely practiced in many countries, including India, China, Japan, Mexico, Peru, and Persia.

In the Middle East, the ancient **civilizations** of the Sumerians and the Babylonians used carved surfaces as **seals** for stamping and impressing marks into clay **tablets**. Paper was invented in the first century, but it was not widely available in Europe until the 15th century. After this time block printing became an important way of reproducing words and illustrations for early books. Artists were involved in drawing the pictures, but skilled craftsmen were responsible for copying the drawings onto blocks, carving, and printing.

▲ *This imprint was made using an ancient Babylonian carved seal. The seal was cylinder-shaped, like a soup can, so it could be rolled over soft clay.*

There are many ways of using block printing. You may wish to print the same **image** over and over again on one sheet. Or you can print the same lone image on different sheets of paper to make a matching set, called a **run**. You may simply want to make a picture, exploring the special effects that can be produced using printing blocks.

◀ *This is an illustration from a 15th-century book. It was printed in Germany using wood blocks. A different block was used for each color.*

4

▲ *Fabrics such as silk and cotton can be decorated with block printed patterns.*

◀ *The famous artist Pablo Picasso block printed this big, bold portrait, called* Woman with a Hat.

To get started you will need the following equipment:

Craft knife
Cutting board
Scissors

Small wooden blocks or empty matchboxes
Modeling clay and rolling pin
Pieces of packing foam
Elmer's Glue-All
Nail polish remover

Printing inks (see page 16)
Poster paints
Paint thinner
Wallpaper paste
Dish soap

Apron and rubber gloves (to protect your skin and clothes)

Metal or glass sheet (such as a baking tray) to use as an inking slab
Large lid or margarine tub and foam sponge to make into a printing pad
Rollers
Paint brushes

Fabric (plain cotton)
Paper and cardboard (a range of types and colors)

Old newspapers (to protect work surfaces)

An old blanket, sheet of plastic wrap, and masking tape to make a printing table

Drying rack or line

Needles, thread, and a sewing machine

Word processor

Sketchbook and camera

BLOCK PRINTING ON FABRIC

In Europe, block printing by hand on fabric was practiced as early as the 13th century. In the 18th and 19th centuries, huge factories were built to produce cloth in large quantities. It became cheaper and easier to print patterns by machine.

In 1881, a British **designer** called William Morris and some of his friends set up a company to revive the craft of hand block printing. The designs for their prints were based on the plants and birds in the countryside around their homes. They also took ideas from **illuminated manuscripts** and other decorative objects from the Middle Ages. The fabric was printed using blocks, but it was so skillfully done that the join lines were almost invisible. Morris's ideas spread to Europe and the United States, where other artists and craftspeople started producing prints using the same kind of hand blocks.

▲ *This fabric print, called* The Strawberry Thief, *was designed by William Morris in 1883.*

A hand block-printed fabric designed ▶
by Phyllis Barron and Dorothy Larcher.

In the 1930s, the British painters Phyllis Barron and Dorothy Larcher took up hand block printing after finding some old printing blocks in a French market. Eventually they set up a printing workshop.

Enid Marx, who learned hand block printing from Barron and Larcher, was very successful. In the 1930s, she designed the fabric for the seats on the London subway system.

In India, a strong **tradition** of hand block printing goes back many centuries. The **technique** is still widely practiced today, and clothes made of Indian hand-printed fabric are sold around the world. Although hand printing takes many hours of work, **wages** in India are low, so cloth can still be produced cheaply.

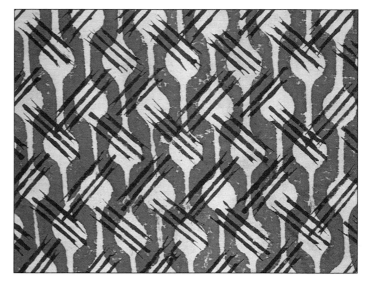

▲ Enid Marx made block prints using bold simple shapes and colors.

▼ This delicate, hand-printed Indian cloth was made in the 19th century.

A detail from a piece of modern block-printed cotton from Rajasthan, northern India. ►

▼ Block printing is a slow, time consuming job.

BLOCK PRINTING ON PAPER

Many artists use the technique of block printing. They make a limited number of prints from the same block. Each print is numbered and signed, and together they make an **edition**.

In Europe, block printing has been used to make pictures and book illustrations since the 15th century. Albrecht Dürer was a skillful German artist and printmaker, working in the late 14th and early 15th centuries. His **woodcuts** have been studied by other artists and have helped them understand the many ways of block printing.

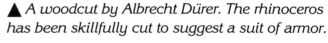 ▲ *A woodcut by Albrecht Dürer. The rhinoceros has been skillfully cut to suggest a suit of armor.*

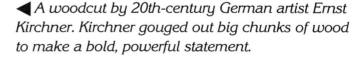 ◀ *A woodcut by 20th-century German artist Ernst Kirchner. Kirchner gouged out big chunks of wood to make a bold, powerful statement.*

Over the centuries, different materials and techniques have been developed. Very hard wood, such as boxwood, can be cut with fine, pointed tools to produce crisp, delicate lines. Soft wood can be cut freely in any direction to give bold, lively designs. Pieces of **linoleum** are used to make linocuts. The design is gouged out of the linoleum to produce bold shapes.

▲ *Hard woods are chosen to make wood engravings. These woods allow the artist to use very sharp tools to cut crisp lines, close together.*

▲ *Linocuts produce strong, bold shapes. This one by Edward Bawden tells the story of* The Ant and the Grasshopper *from* Aesop's Fables.

In the 19th century, hand **presses** were used to make posters with words and pictures. The letters were created from individual pieces of wooden **type**. The illustrations were **engraved** in wooden blocks.

Often, prints are deliberately made using only one color—usually black ink on white paper. A special feature of block printing is that the spaces between the shapes are as important as the shapes themselves. The strong contrast between black and white shows this design feature at its best.

▲ *In the 18th and 19th centuries, the Japanese made beautiful, multicolored prints.*

The Japanese have a long tradition of colored block printing. Prints were made using a number of blocks inked up with different colors. Each block was printed one on top of the other to create a multicolored picture. A whole team of experts was involved in the process.

FINDING PRINTING BLOCKS

There are many things that you can use as printing blocks. Look around your house, garden, classroom, and school grounds. Look for things with an interesting surface or **texture**.

TURN TO PAGES 16-17 TO FIND OUT ABOUT INKING UP YOUR PRINTING BLOCK.

1 Find objects that can be used as printing blocks. Your hand, a piece of crushed paper, a block of rough wood, a bulldog clip, a cork, or a piece of sponge will work.

2 Experiment with vegetables and fruit. For example, cut an apple, pear, or onion in half, lengthwise or widthwise. Wipe the surface dry with a piece of paper towel and ink it up.

3 The firm flesh of a potato can be carved to make a printing block. Cut a potato in half and use a craft knife to cut away parts of the flesh.

Keep the shapes big and bold. Dry the surface carefully before inking and printing. If it is too wet the ink will not take.

Remember: always be careful when using a craft knife.

PAGES 28-29 SHOW YOU HOW TO USE YOUR BLOCK TO MAKE REPEATING PATTERNS.

MAKING PRINTING BLOCKS

Many objects have interesting shapes and textures, but they are too flat or flimsy to use just as you find them. If you want to print with feathers, leaves, keys, pieces of lace, wire mesh, or burlap, you will need to mount them first.

MAKING A BLOCK USING FOUND OBJECTS

1 Find a block of wood or a small box, such as a matchbox.

2 Cover the surface with glue. Use good, strong glue, such as Elmer's Glue-All.

3 Place the object you want to print on the glue and let it dry thoroughly.

TURN TO PAGES 16-17 TO FIND OUT ABOUT INKING UP YOUR PRINTING BLOCKS.

DESIGNING AND MAKING YOUR OWN BLOCKS

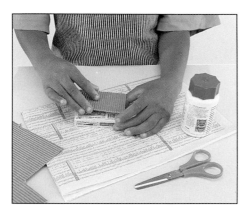

1 Find things that will give a raised surface when stuck on a block—for example, toothpicks, pieces of spaghetti, or a length of string.

2 Experiment with different ways of arranging them.

3 When you are pleased with the picture or pattern you have designed, cover the surface of a block of wood with glue and stick the pieces in place. Make several blocks and build up patterns.

PAGES 28-29 SHOW YOU HOW TO USE YOUR BLOCKS TO MAKE REPEATING PATTERNS.

MAKING A PAPER BLOCK

1 Take a piece of thin cardboard for the base of the block.

3 Glue the layers down firmly on the base, one on top of the other.

5 Take a print by laying a sheet of paper on the block and rolling over the back of the paper firmly with a clean roller.

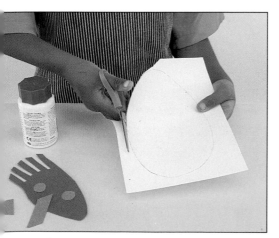

2 Cut strong, simple shapes and bold lines from construction paper.

4 Ink up the block using oil-based inks. Do not use water-based inks.

MAKING CUT-OUT BLOCKS

STYROFOAM BLOCKS

1 Find some blocks of Styrofoam. You need the kind used to pack new electrical equipment, such as radios and refrigerators.

2 Paint a design on a piece of Styrofoam with nail polish remover. **Be careful not to spill any.** The nail polish remover will dissolve any areas of the Styrofoam it touches.

3 Ink up the block. The pattern you made will show up as white space. The remaining surface will print in color.

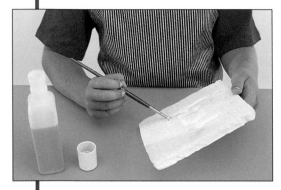

CARVED POTATOES

shown on page 11, where parts of the potato are cut away to make a raised block.

Remember: always be careful when using a craft knife.

Cut a potato in half and use a craft knife to carve shapes into the surface. The design you cut out won't show. This is different from the potato block

CLAY BLOCKS

1 Use a glass bottle or an old rolling pin to roll out a block of modeling clay about one inch deep. Make the block as flat and level as you can.

2 Cut the block to any size and shape you want with a table knife.

3 Press objects with interesting shapes firmly into the clay block. For example, use screws, wire, wire mesh, keys, paperclips, or buttons. When you remove each object its shape will be pressed into the clay.

4 Ink the block and make a print. You'll get a negative image of the object.

Note: Modeling clay is greasy. It can reject water-based ink. Mixing the ink with dish soap helps.

PRINTING INKS AND PAINTS

Printing ink is available in tubes or tubs from art stores. Use a roller to apply color to your block so it spreads out thinly and evenly.

There are two kinds of printing inks: water-based and oil-based. Water-based inks are easily cleaned from the block, but oil-based inks have to be cleaned off with paint thinner. If your block is at all greasy it will repel water-based ink. You can avoid this problem by mixing a little dish soap into the ink.

Paint is a good substitute for printing ink, particularly when you are using your block as a stamp. Mix poster paint with a little wallpaper paste. Do not use paint with cardboard or paper blocks. It will make them get soggy and fall apart.

"Inking up" is the special term used for covering the printing block with ink or paint. You can ink up a block using a brush, roller, or pad.

MAKING AN INK PAD

1 Find a large lid or margarine tub. Cut a layer of foam sponge to fit.

2 Put the ink or paint into the container. Leave it for a few minutes. The sponge will soak up the ink.

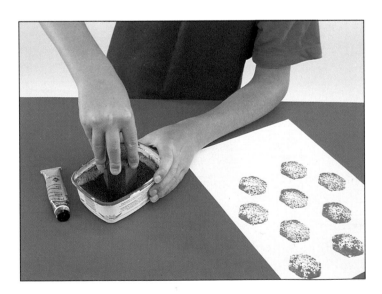

3 Press your block down on the pad. It will take up an even coating of ink, ready for printing.

4 Prepare a different printing pad for each color you are going to use.

Using a Roller

4 Roll the ink smoothly onto the block.

5 Place a sheet of paper on the block and roll over it with a clean roller.

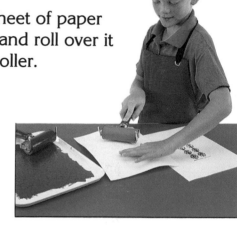

6 Prepare a different inking slab for each color you use.

1 Use a smooth, flat sheet of glass or metal (an old baking tray will do) as an inking slab. Put it on a pad of old newspapers.

2 Put a small dot of ink on the slab. Remember that you always need much less ink than you think. Roll it out thinly and evenly to cover the slab.

3 Now you are ready to ink up your block. The roller will have a thin, even coat of ink on it.

COLOR PRINTING

You may wish to print a design using more than one color. The easiest way to do this is to use two or more printing blocks, inked with different colors, to make a repeating pattern.

Another method is to overprint the image several times in different colors. For this you need several different blocks, all the same size. You can also overprint using the same block by gradually cutting away different parts of the design. A different color is used after each cut. The problem with this method is that it destroys the block.

If you are going to overprint using several blocks, you must make sure they all print exactly on top of each other. If the blocks are not properly **registered**, the image will be blurred.

▲ *This print was made using half a rutabaga. The rutabaga was cut into, inked up with different colors, and overprinted several times.*

OVERPRINTING

1 Make an accurate color drawing of how you want your finished print to look.

2 Make several tracings from the drawing, one for each color. Place the sheets of tracing paper on top of each other. They should line up exactly.

3 From the tracings, make the blocks you need.

4 Cut a cardboard base about one inch bigger all around than your printing blocks.

5 Cut a second piece of cardboard to the same size. Place a block in the center and trace it. Cut along the lines to make a hole exactly the same size as your printing blocks. Glue this cardboard onto the base.

6 Ink up the first block and place it in the cardboard mount you have just made.

7 Using a piece of printing paper cut to exactly the same size as the mount, take a print of the first block.

8 Ink up the second block and place it in the mount. Again, position your printing paper exactly on the mount and take a print.

9 Do the same with the third block.

PRINTING ON FABRIC

1 Choose a plain fabric with a close **weave**. Cotton fabric, such as unbleached calico, gives good results.

2 Wash the fabric carefully and let it dry. This is important if the fabric is new, because the **finish** put on at the factory may keep the ink from taking evenly.

3 Prepare a printing table. Cover a table top with an old blanket. Wrap it over the edges and fasten it underneath. Cover this with a sheet of plastic wrap and layers of newspaper.

4 Tape the fabric you are going to print to the newspaper with masking tape. Make sure it is flat and unwrinkled.

5 Use special fabric printing ink (available from art stores), or the same printing ink or paint-and-paste mixture used for paper (see page 16). If you are making something that you will want to wash, you will need to choose a waterproof, oil-based ink.

8 Start by making something fairly small, such as a scarf or handkerchief. Once you have got the idea, go on to print enough fabric to make an apron or cushion covers.

To print a ▶ *large piece of fabric, such as a tablecloth, fold the cloth and iron in the folds. This will help you print in straight lines.*

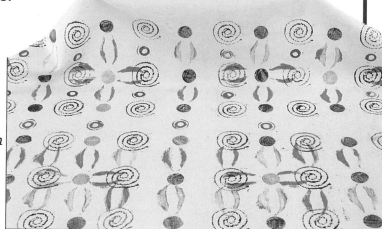

6 Use any of the different sorts of printing blocks described on pages 10-15. Clay blocks are particularly suitable for use on fabric. Fruit and vegetable blocks give good results. Prints are always stamped onto fabric: the blocks are placed ink-side down on the cloth.

7 To print a large piece of fabric, it is helpful to use a block that can be mounted on wood so it lasts longer. It may help to use a wooden mallet to tap the block down lightly onto the fabric.

▼ *Some of the things you can make using block printed fabric include (clockwise from top) a pillow cover, a long silk scarf, a cotton handkerchief, and a square silk scarf.*

TURN TO PAGES 24-25 FOR IDEAS ABOUT USING PRINTED FABRIC.

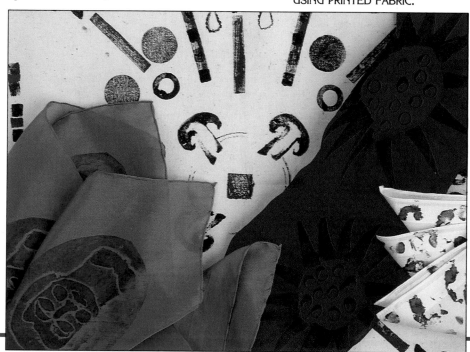

PROJECTS USING PAPER

Collect a range of different paper. Some will be ideal for printing wrapping paper, others for cards or posters.

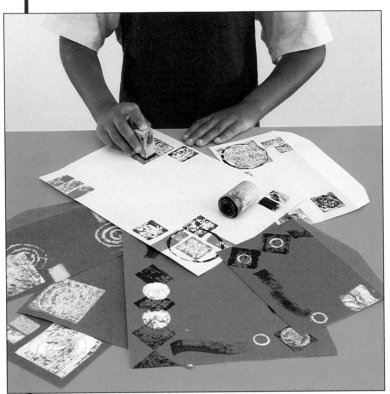

2 Make greetings cards by printing on stiff paper or cardboard folded in half. If you want to make a large number of cards, say for a holiday, set up a **production team** (see posters project on page 23).

1 Print yor own writing paper and envelopes. Print borders on the writing paper, leaving enough space for writing. Envelopes can have a more overall design, but leave space for the address. Also, try using a word processor to design and print a heading for the writing paper. Then print the borders.

3 Make wrapping paper and matching gift tags. Use a printing block to build up a repeating pattern for the wrapping paper. Turn to pages 28-29 for ideas about building up patterns. Make matching gift tags by printing the same design onto cardboard. Or cut a piece off the bottom of the printed sheet and tape it onto cardboard.

POSTERS

1 With a group of friends, make a poster to advertise a special event, such as a play, concert, or tag sale. Organize yourselves into a production team to design and print an edition of about ten posters.

2 Decide what the poster needs to say. Use as few words as possible, but be sure to include all the important details: the name of the event, the date, the time, the address, where to get tickets, the cost, and so on.

3 Discuss how you can use block printing to make the posters look attractive. Make several designs and discuss which one will work best. Leave a space in the center to put the text.

4 Use a word processor to write the text. Print it out and enlarge the type on a photocopier to the size you need. Make ten copies.

5 Print the design onto the poster. Organize yourselves into an **assembly line**, with different people responsible for printing the different colors in the design. Put the text in the center of each poster.

Wed. September 3rd

HARVEST SUPPER

6 p.m. in the
FIRE HALL
Tickets $6.00 from
Mrs. Patel 555-2304

A PROJECT USING FABRIC

Gather together a group of friends to make curtains. These could be for a room in your school, or for some other local public building. Do not choose a very large window. In your group, include someone who is good at math, someone with good design skills, and someone who can sew.

MAKING A PAIR OF BLOCK-PRINTED CURTAINS

1 Visit the room with your team. Discuss who uses the room, when, and why. Try to talk to these people about what they like. Look at the colors in the room. With all of this in mind, discuss the design and colors for the curtains.

2 Draw up several ideas. Make blocks for the idea you like best. Test it out by printing it on paper.

3 Decide how much fabric you will need. Take careful measurements of the window. Measure the length from top to bottom of the frame, then add 16 inches. This will allow for hems at the top and bottom, plus extra to make sure the finished curtains cover the frame well.

Measurements for each curtain:

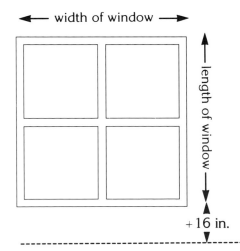

width of window

length of window

+16 in.

4 Measure the width of the window. Curtains look best if they are gathered in folds, so for a pair of curtains, make sure each one is at least the width of the window. Fabric is sold in standard widths. Most windows will need two widths of fabric sewn together to make each curtain.

5 Multiply the number of widths you need by the length of the window. This gives the length of fabric needed.

6 Now work out the cost of the project. Multiply the cost of the fabric per yard by the number of yards you need. **Estimate** how many tubes of printing ink you will need.

7 Now that you have a design and a cost, discuss the project with a responsible adult to get approval. Agree on a plan to pay for the project.

8 Prepare a large printing table and print all the fabric you need.

9 Now sew the curtains. If you are using two widths for each curtain, sew them together, matching the patterns carefully. Hem the sides.

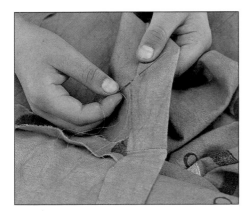

10 Turn under the top edge, and pin on some curtain heading tape. Sew it in place with a sewing machine.

11 Attach curtain hooks and put the curtains up. Allow them to hang for a week. Then pin up and hem the bottom.

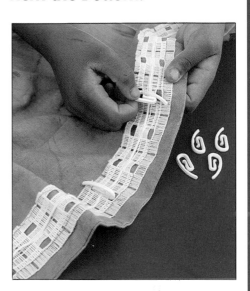

THE GALLERY

Look around to get ideas for print designs. Look for bold shapes and objects that will give crisp, clean results. Make sketches and take photographs of the things you see.

On pages 10-15 there are suggestions for objects to collect and make into printing blocks. The pictures here give some ideas for patterns to print with blocks.

▲ *A row of railings.*

▼ *Brickwork.*

▲ *Ducks against the setting sun.*

A bunch of grapes. ▶

▲ *Straight lines of cut wheat.*

◀ *Holes in a metal bench.*

A spotted fish. ▶

▼ *Bold strawberry shapes.*

MAKING PATTERNS

Once you have designed and made a printing block, you can start experimenting with it to build up regular and **random** patterns.

First, experiment by repeating a single block, using one color only. The amount of white space between the prints is very important. The same block can give very different results, depending on how close together you place the repeats. Also, each print you make will be slightly different. Sometimes it will be full of ink, sometimes it will be dry. This all adds to the effect. Here are some different ways of building up patterns.

◀ *Random repeats.*

Half-drop repeats. ▶

▼ *Regular repeats.*

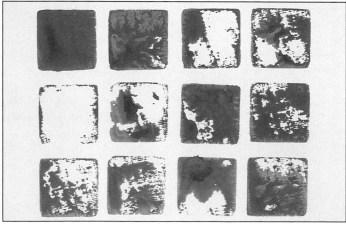

▼ *Square brick repeats.*

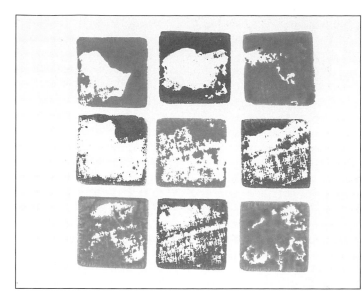

▲ Now try introducing a second color.

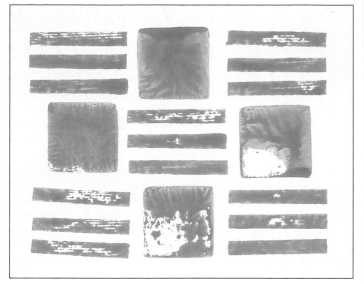

▲ Introduce a second printing block.

This panel was made using six different blocks and overprinting them in different colors. With block printing, you can overprint light colors on dark ink. ▶

GLOSSARY

Assembly line A group of people working together to get a job done quickly, as in a factory. Each person is responsible for a stage of the process.

Civilizations Groups of people who form a state with a highly organized structure and culture. Civilizations that existed thousands of years ago are called ancient civilizations.

Designer A person who works out the shape and style of an object or decoration.

Edition In printing, an edition is the entire group of copies made.

Engraved Carved into a block of wood or metal plate so that a print can be made.

Estimate Calculate roughly.

Fabric Cloth.

Finish A special surface put on a piece of cloth, to change the way it looks or feels.

Illuminated manuscripts Books written out by hand and highly decorated. They were made in the Middle Ages, before people knew how to print books.

Image Picture.

Linoleum A floor covering made of canvas coated with solid linseed oil.

Presses Machines used for printing.

Production team A group of people, each with special skills, who work together to design and make something.

Random Without any plan or order.

Registered Correctly lined up.

Run A number of prints from the same block or blocks.

Seals Small, carved objects that can be pressed into a soft substance to make a mark.

Tablets Slabs of stone, clay, or wood. In the past they were used as writing surfaces.

Technique Method or skill.

Texture The feel of an object's surface.

Tradition A custom that has been practiced over many years, by one generation of people after another.

Type A small block of metal or wood with a letter on it, used for printing words.

Wages The money a worker earns.

Weave The pattern made by weaving. This is a method of making fabric on a loom by pushing cross threads under and over vertical threads.

Woodcuts Prints made using a block of wood that has a design carved into it.

FURTHER INFORMATION

BOOKS TO READ

Better Homes and Gardens Incredibly Awesome Crafts for Kids (Des Moines, Iowa, 1992).

Devonshire, Hilary. *Printing* (New York: Franklin Watts, 1988).

Haddad, Helen R. *Potato Printing* (New York: Harper Collins, 1981).

Reader's Digest Crafts and Hobbies (Pleasantville, N.Y.: Reader's Digest, 1979).

For further information about arts and crafts, write to the following organization:

American Craft Council
72 Spring Street
New York, NY 10012

INDEX

ACKNOWLEDGMENTS

The publishers would like to thank the following for allowing their photographs to be reproduced: Bridgeman Art Library 5 left, 6 left, 7 bottom left, 8 bottom, 9 top left (Chelmsford Museums Service); E. T. Archive 4 bottom, 8 top, 9 top right, 9 bottom; Eye Ubiquitous title page, 7 center right, 7 bottom right (L. Goffin), 26 top right (P. Prestidge), 27 bottom left; Holburne Museum and Crafts Study Centre, Bath 6 right, 7 top; Michael Holford 4 top; Tony Stone Worldwide 5 right (Osmond), 26 left (C. Harvey), 26 center (G. Kohler), 26 right (D. Bassett), 27 top (A. Sacks); Zefa 27 center right (R. Morsch), 27 bottom right (L. Lefever). All other photographs, including cover, were supplied by Zul Mukhida. Logo artwork was supplied by John Yates.

The linocut *Woman with a Hat*, by Pablo Picasso, appears by permission of the copyright holders © DACS 1993.

The fabric prints *Winchester*, by Phyllis Barron and Dorothy Larcher, and *Hail*, by Enid Marx, appear by permission of the Holburne Museum and Crafts Study Centre, Bath.

The linocut *The Ant and the Grasshopper*, by Edward Bawden, appears by permission of the estate of Edward Bawden.